50th Anniversary—Special Edition

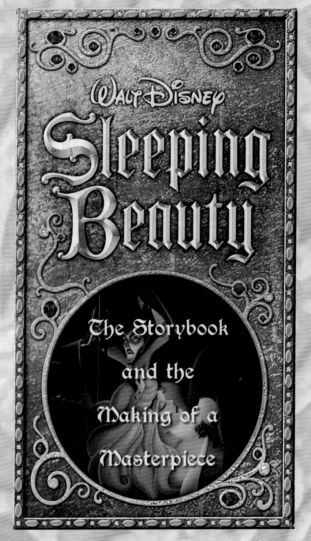

Walt Disney

Sleeping Beauty

The Storybook
and the
Making of a
Masterpiece

DISNEY
EDITIONS

Academy Award® is a registered trademark and service
mark of the Academy of Motion Picture Arts and Sciences.

CinemaScope® is a registered trademark of
Twentieth Century Fox Film Corporation.

Grammy® Award is a registered trademark and
service mark of The Recording Academy.

Technirama® is a registered trademark
of Technicolor by Thomson.

For information address Disney Editions,
114 Fifth Avenue, New York, New York 10011-5690.

Disney Editions Editorial Director: Wendy Lefkon
Disney Editions Senior Editor: Jody Revenson
Disney Editions Assistant Editor: Jessica Ward

Produced by Welcome Enterprises, Inc.
6 West 18th Street, New York, NY 10011

Written by Jeff Kurtti
Designed by NightandDayDesign.biz

Printed in Canada

FIRST EDITION

ISBN 978-1-4231-1917-3

Library of Congress Catalog Card Number on file.

Visit www.disneybooks.com

Contents

The History

The History

A princess in peril, a handsome prince, a magic spell, and a powerful villain—all the elements of a classic fairy tale. Several classic fairy tales, in fact. Walt Disney had already created beloved animated features around two similar legends with *Snow White and the Seven Dwarfs* (1937) and *Cinderella* (1950) when he and his studio team embarked on another animated feature project with its roots in a well-known story, this time that of "the sleeping beauty."

There are, as with all fairy tales, various and many retellings of the legend of the drowsing princess in various media over many years.

Left: Sleeping Beauty's *original 1959 movie poster. Above:* Sleeping Beauty *was translated into many languages, including German.*

ℒiterary ℒegacy

No one knows the precise origins of the Sleeping Beauty story, but the earliest published version appears to be in the fourteenth century Catalan *Frayre de*

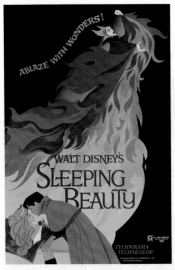

Joy e Sor de Placer. A similar story appeared under the title "Troylus and Zellandine" in the sixteenth-century French *Perceforest*. There is evidence of even older retellings in Arabic and Chinese.

Under the title "Sole, Luna, e Talia" ("Sun, Moon, and Talia") a variation of the legend was published in 1634 in Giambattista Basile's *Pentamerone*; the Brothers Jacob and Wilhelm Grimm published their version, "Dornröschen" ("Briar Rose") in the 1812-1815 volumes *Kinder- und Hausmärchen* (*Children's and Household Tales*).

Above: A Sleeping Beauty *movie poster. Right: Early concept drawings for royal characters, such as King Stefan and King Hubert.*

But perhaps the most famous telling is "La Belle au Bois dormant" ("The Sleeping Beauty in the Wood") set down by Charles Perrault and published in 1697 in *Histoires ou Contes du Temps passé* (*Tales and Stories of Times Past*). The best-known fairy tale collection of its day, the volume also features distinctive versions of "Little Red Riding Hood," "Bluebeard," "Cinderella," "Tom Thumb," and "Puss in Boots." J. R. R. Tolkien once noted that this volume remains so influential that, when asked to name a fairy tale, most people will cite one of the stories in Perrault's collection.

KING STEFAN. CHRISTENING.

KING HUPERT. SCENE WITH PHILLIP.

The Disney Version

With *Sleeping Beauty*, Walt Disney realised that he could not merely repeat the successes of *Snow White* and *Cinderella*. Instead, he sought to create the pinnacle of the animated art form. In seeking a whole new approach to telling a classic tale, Walt and his staff created an innovative design approach, a sophistication of musical storytelling, and a quality of character animation that can certainly be considered decades ahead of its time, but also as timeless as the original tale itself.

Thus, the story behind the story of *Sleeping Beauty* rarely seems to live "happily ever after," for there is always a new take on a venerable old tale, and always a new and appreciative audience ready to venture into its many wonders.

Above: Prince Phillip awakens Princess Aurora. Right: Over the last half century, Sleeping Beauty *has become a Walt Disney classic.*

In a faraway land, long ago, lived a king and his fair queen. For many years they had longed for a child, and finally their wish was granted. A daughter was born, and they called her Aurora.

Thus a holiday was proclaimed,
and the entire kingdom gathered to
celebrate the long-awaited royal birth.

16

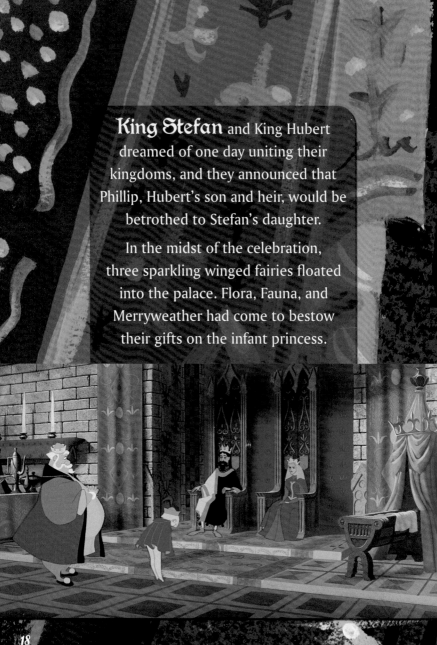

King Stefan and King Hubert dreamed of one day uniting their kingdoms, and they announced that Phillip, Hubert's son and heir, would be betrothed to Stefan's daughter.

In the midst of the celebration, three sparkling winged fairies floated into the palace. Flora, Fauna, and Merryweather had come to bestow their gifts on the infant princess.

Flora offered the gift of beauty;

Fauna, the gift of song;

but as Merryweather began
                to present her gift . . .

BOOOOM!

Maleficent, a wicked fairy, burst into the hall in a blaze of green flames. Angry that she had not been invited to the celebration, she placed a curse on the tiny princess.

"Before the sun sets on her sixteenth birthday," Maleficent promised, "she shall prick her finger on the spindle of a spinning wheel . . . and die!"

Then, with a malicious cackle,
the evil fairy disappeared.

Merryweather's powers were not strong enough to undo Maleficent's curse, but she could *change* it.

Not in death, but just in sleep,
the fateful prophecy you'll keep.

And from this slumber you shall wake,
when true love's kiss the spell shall break.

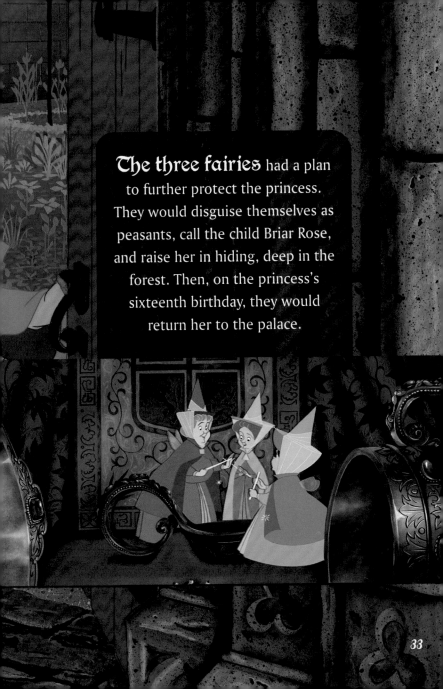

The three fairies had a plan
to further protect the princess.
They would disguise themselves as
peasants, call the child Briar Rose,
and raise her in hiding, deep in the
forest. Then, on the princess's
sixteenth birthday, they would
return her to the palace.

Year after year, Maleficent's henchmen scoured the kingdom for the princess without success.

As Aurora's sixteenth birthday neared, Maleficent realised that for all those years, her henchmen had been searching for a baby! The angry villain hastily dispatched her pet raven to search for the princess, now a young maiden.

On the morning of the princess's sixteenth birthday, Flora, Fauna, and Merryweather made plans for a party—with a real birthday cake and a dress a princess could be proud of.

𝕿o make their surprise
complete, they sent Briar Rose
out to pick wild berries.

The maiden wandered through
the forest singing, her sweet voice
drifting through the trees.

45

Prince Phillip was riding nearby, and he heard her lovely song. She did not hear the prince approach until he joined in her singing and took her hand.

Without knowing who the other was, the prince and Briar Rose fell instantly in love, and they planned to meet later that night.

But then, Maleficent's pet raven flew overhead. He raced to the Forbidden Mountain to tell his mistress.

Back at the cottage, Briar Rose told the fairies all about the handsome stranger she had met, and they realised that she was in love. They knew the time had come to tell her the truth.

As they began their long journey back to the palace, all Aurora could think of was the young man she had met that day and how she would never see him again.

When they reached the palace, the fairies left Aurora in a small room. A sinister, green wisp of light appeared. In a trance, the princess followed it through a secret panel. The fairies returned just in time to see Aurora step into a dark passageway.

In the middle of a small room at the top of a tower, the green light stopped and transformed into a spinning wheel.

Aurora, still in a trance, pricked her finger on the wheel's sharp spindle and fell to the floor. Maleficent stood over the fallen princess, laughing cruelly at the villainous victory.

The fairies knew the king and queen would be heartbroken, so they drifted all about the palace, putting everyone into a deep sleep.

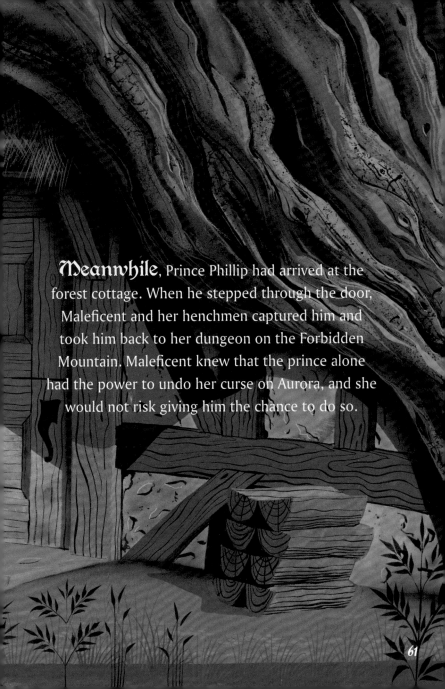

Meanwhile, Prince Phillip had arrived at the forest cottage. When he stepped through the door, Maleficent and her henchmen captured him and took him back to her dungeon on the Forbidden Mountain. Maleficent knew that the prince alone had the power to undo her curse on Aurora, and she would not risk giving him the chance to do so.

Realising that Aurora's mysterious young man must be Phillip, the fairies rushed back to the cottage, but they found only the signs of a violent struggle and Prince Phillip's cap. They raced away toward the darkness of Maleficent's mountain lair.

In the dungeon, Maleficent revealed to the prince that the girl he had fallen in love with was Princess Aurora. The evil fairy told Prince Phillip that only he could awaken Aurora—with a kiss. Phillip knew he must somehow escape and save his true love.

When Maleficent departed, the good
fairies appeared and released the prince, arming
him with the enchanted Shield of Virtue and the
mighty Sword of Truth. The prince made his way
through the courtyard, swiftly mounted his horse,
and fled toward the drawbridge.

As Phillip neared Stefan's palace,
Maleficent cast a spell. A wall of thick,
thorny vines appeared, and soon the
prince was surrounded. He made quick
work of the twining branches, using the
Sword of Truth to clear a path.

When the prince neared the
castle bridge, Maleficent appeared in
a ball of fire right in front of him.
Then she turned herself into a huge
dragon and blasted him with
red-hot flames.

Phillip defended himself with the Shield of Virtue. He took aim with his sword and hurled it at the dragon. The beast fell back and plunged over the edge of a cliff. Maleficent was gone. The thorny vines dissolved into the ground, and the fire and smoke vanished.

Prince Phillip ran through the castle gates and up the stairs, to the chamber where Aurora lay. He knelt beside the princess and kissed her. . . .

The sleeping beauty awakened.

75

The spell broken,

everyone else in

the kingdom awoke.

In the throne room, all eyes
focused on the top of the grand stairway.
Prince Phillip and Princess Aurora appeared
arm in arm, beaming with joy.

Soon, the court musicians struck up a
dance, and Prince Phillip whisked the
princess away to the dance floor.

As all the palace court watched,
Princess Aurora and Prince Phillip
danced in each other's arms. . . .

And they lived happily ever after. . . .

The Production

The Production

Although Walt Disney, even in the 1950s, had a reputation as a "fairy-tale teller"—often called a "modern Aesop" or "today's Hans Christian Andersen"—he had, at the time, only translated two fairy tales into animated features: *Snow White and the Seven Dwarfs* in 1937 and *Cinderella* in 1950.

Nevertheless, *Sleeping Beauty* was a curious choice for the Studio to proceed with in the early 1950s, most simply because some of the criticism of *Cinderella* had to do with its story similarities to *Snow White*. Disney registered the title *Sleeping Beauty* with the Motion Picture Association of America on January 19, 1950, a month before the release of *Cinderella*.

Left: Drawing of Prince Phillip awakening Princess Aurora was inspired by live models (above) acting out the scene.

It can only be conjectured that the quality of
Cinderella and the reaction of preview audiences might
have prompted the registration of this title for safety's
sake. But Disney storyman Joe Grant recalled doing
work on *Sleeping Beauty* as early as the late 1930s, at
the same time that *Peter Pan* and *Alice in Wonderland*
as well as "The Little Mermaid" and several other
Hans Christian Andersen stories were being looked at,
too. So it's apparent that the canon of fairy tales and
children's literature was *always* being examined and re-
examined for future feature development at Disney.

"You've got a lot of elements to consider," Walt said. "For one thing, you fight to do something that breaks away from what we've done before. *Sleeping Beauty* was tough, because it had a lot of the elements that we had in *Snow White* and *Cinderella*. You've got to give the animators new things to work on to keep their enthusiasm up. All of a sudden in a meeting one of them will say, 'Haven't we done this before?' And we have, so we have to change it all over again."

Left: Live models portrayed characters, such as the three good fairies, to help artists see how the animated characters (above) should move.

From Fable to Feature

Challenges aside, development of the film began in earnest in 1951, and by 1952 a full storyboard had been completed. Ted Sears, Winston Hibler, Bill Peet, and Ralph Wright contributed to the story. Songwriters Sammy Fain and Jack Lawrence had developed a series of original songs, including "Holiday," "Mirage," and "Sunbeams in Your Pocket."

In this version, the princess was something of a "poor little rich girl," growing up discontent in her castle and burdened by her royal pedigree. The character was much the same as Princess Jasmine would be in *Aladdin* decades later. The characters and design were not terribly distinctive or remarkable. The fairies, even Maleficent, were depicted as gnome- or pixielike creatures.

Left: Supervising director Eric Larson, storymen Joe Rinaldi and Don DaGradi, and animator Marc Davis discuss storyboards. Right: Early concepts of Maleficent depicted her with antennae to make her seem less human.

This early version just didn't seem to wholly satisfy anyone, particularly Walt, and some of the innate structure of the source story impeded the flow of action, character development, and motion-picture story.

The story team finally threw out the first version and started over again, keeping the bare elements of the legend and developing the story to suit the needs of the film.

Although the Disney version of *Sleeping Beauty* offers full screen credit and promotional recognition to Charles Perrault's version of the tale, it is actually closer to the Brothers Grimm retelling of the famous story.

The Grimm tale ends earlier than the others, when the princess awakens with the prince's kiss. In the Perrault version, the awakening of the princess is only the halfway point. Perrault continues the narrative in what becomes a very grisly story, indeed.

Left and above: Many styles were explored for Princess Aurora. Artist Tom Oreb's concept, inspired by actress Audrey Hepburn, ultimately became the backbone of the character's appearance.

A Grim Perrault Tale

The prince and Aurora are covertly wed, and the princess bears him two children, which he keeps secret from the Queen. The Queen, it unfortunately turns out, is of ogre lineage. Once the prince accedes to the throne, he brings Aurora and the children to his kingdom but promptly leaves to make war on his neighbour, the Emperor Contalabutte. This neatly leaves the ogre Queen Mother in charge.

The ogre Queen sends Aurora and the children to a secluded lodge deep in the woods. This is where things get gruesome. The Queen orders the royal chef

there to cook the boy with a lovely Sauce Robert, for her dinner. The compassionate cook substitutes lamb, which fools the ogre Queen. Naturally, the queen then demands a meal made of the girl, but is likewise fooled when the chef prepares a young goat in the same delicious sauce.

When the ogre Queen next demands that the chef serve up a meal of Princess Aurora *à la Robert*, she is fooled once again with a hind prepared in the same fashion. Soon, however, she discovers the trick and orders a large vat in the castle courtyard filled with vipers and other poisonous and unpleasant creatures. The prince returns just in the nick of time, and the ogre Queen, revealed for her evils, throws herself into the vile pit she has prepared for the others and is painfully and graphically eradicated. Everyone else, it is presumed, lives happily ever after.

Left: Initial concept for the three good fairies' cottage in the forest.

Above: This early idea for Maleficent includes her outfit's spiky collar.

Streamlining the Story

Walt Disney is often praised for his storytelling abilities, but in many cases, it is his skill as a story *editor* that is even more important. Sometimes, the choices made in adapting a tale have less to do with what is left in than with what is left out.

Part of the difficulty with the Sleeping Beauty story was in trying to develop a third, and yet distinct, "princess in peril." What could they do to make Princess Aurora, whose plight is so similar to Snow White's and Cinderella's, *different* from them?

First of all, the story removes the princess's knowledge of her own plight—she has no idea she's in danger. In that way, she can be treated simply as a person or a personality, since there is no requirement to inform the character's actions or behaviour through her predicament. This meant that ultimately Aurora was given an entirely different personality, with a fresh and modern sensibility that made her more appealing.

Left: Sleeping Beauty's supervising director, Eric Larson, reviews the storyboard for the film's pivotal spinning-wheel scene.

The hundred-year sleep of the fairy tale becomes a sort of hasty slumber party, probably due to Walt's propensity for thinking rhythmically and cinematically. And though some of the plot logic is a little irrational in places—the fairies abstain from using magic for sixteen years and then use it on the eve of Aurora's birthday to bake a cake—on the whole, the Disney team took the memorable icons of a half-remembered fairy tale and made them into a story that *appears* traditional, and yet is distinctly Disney.

Prolonged Production

"When you ask Walt Disney how long *Sleeping Beauty* was in the works," Bob Thomas reported in 1958, "he will give you the reply, 'Too long.'"

When it finally premiered on January 29, 1959, Walt Disney's *Sleeping Beauty* had been in active production from 1951 until the end of 1958, setting a record for being the Disney animated film with the longest production schedule.

Part of the reason for the lengthy production schedule and high overall expense of *Sleeping Beauty* had to do with what the Studio staff sometimes called "The Deluge"—all the work in television, film, and the building of Disneyland that hit in 1954. This limited both the resources of the Studio and its staff, as well as the availability of Walt Disney himself for each individual project.

Although Walt's attention was very much divided during the production of the film, it would be an

Left: Eyvind Earle's modernist concept of Prince Phillip facing Maleficent's castle. Notice the dim sun and eclipsed moon in the background, representing Maleficent's dark control over nature.

injustice to say that he paid no attention to *Sleeping Beauty*. It has been noted that Walt was an instinctive storyteller, and the evidence from his onscreen appearances indicates a fairly polished performer. Walt himself said that he really wanted to direct live-action films, but by the time he had the opportunity to do so, his career had taken him into a whole different realm.

In *Sleeping Beauty*, however, his story skill and directorial adeptness were still much in use. For example, in the original scene following Phillip's abduction by Maleficent and her "goons," the fairies merely gasped at the sight of Phillip's hat in the cottage, and then the scene dissolved to Maleficent baiting Phillip in the dungeon.

Walt said, "I think we can improve the scene by stretching it out a little. It will not only make the story point clearer, but put over some personality. We can get some thought process into the fairies and make them more sympathetic by their taking on something that is beyond their powers—fighting Maleficent." Walt himself supplied the lines of dialogue and worked with Ollie Johnston on the timing of the scene—and it

does everything Walt is quoted as wanting. The fairies became players, as opposed to observers, in Phillip's rescue:

> *Fairies: Maleficent!*
> *Merryweather: She's got Prince Phillip!*
> *Flora: At the Forbidden Mountain.*
> *Fauna: But we can't! We can't go there!*
> *Flora: We can, and we must.*

It's another example of Walt being the "Last Word," just as he had been on every other film, and during every critical juncture of *Sleeping Beauty*.

The Art

The Art

Walt Disney's animated adaptation of *Sleeping Beauty* features one of the most unique and timeless visual designs in the history of cinema. No Disney feature had ever been entrusted to the vision of a single artist, and no feature had been so thoroughly and deeply researched and designed in order to arrive at a distinct and meticulous visual style.

In the publicity for *Sleeping Beauty*, its art design was touted as an attempt to bring life to static forms of fine art; it was often called a "moving painting," or a "living mural."

Left: Eyvind Earle's modern artistic style was chosen by Walt Disney (far right) as the overall look and feel for Sleeping Beauty.

Left: Concepts for the dreamy gift-giving sequences of Sleeping Beauty *contrast well with the strong vertical and horizontal lines used as the backdrop (above) for the rest of the movie.*

Eyvind Earle's paintings of Prince Phillip's escape from Maleficent's castle were instrumental in shaping the final film.

Above: This painting used a mushroom cloud like that from an atomic bomb to make Maleficent's transformation into a dragon seem even more menacing. Right: Sleeping Beauty's *designs were created to look like a mediaeval tapestry.*

Design and Dissent

Eyvind Earle (1916-2000) was the primary motivating force in this design. He joined Disney in 1951 and contributed to the design of several eccentric Disney shorts, such as *Adventures in Music: Melody* (1953), *Adventures in Music: Toot, Whistle, Plunk, and Boom* (1953), *Pigs is Pigs* (1954), and *Paul Bunyan* (1958), before being assigned to supervise the overall design of *Sleeping Beauty*.

"I started by using the best that was in art prior to the Renaissance," the artist explained in 1958. "I studied French, German, Flemish, and Italian art of that period, and especially Albrecht Dürer, Pieter Brueghel, and Huybrecht Van Eyck. Also Botticelli."

Left: Eyvind Earle reviews some of his paintings. Above: Earle used flat shapes and patterns for the nobility and gentry in the backgrounds.

From there, the artist also incorporated Persian miniatures and Japanese prints. The two-dimensional quality of these inspirations served to keep all the visual elements in focus simultaneously, one of the unique qualities of the film that sets it apart from the style of previous, more "realistic" designs.

Above: Backdrops for Sleeping Beauty *were so complex that it took a week to ten days to paint just one. A single background in a more conventional film of the era was usually completed in a day.*

"You know in live-action pictures how the camera focuses on a figure, and the scenery in the background becomes blurred," Earle said. "But that isn't the way you see things in real life. You can look at my face and then look at the mountain behind me a moment later and both will be in focus. So it is with *Sleeping Beauty*. Everything from the foreground to the far distance is in focus. That gives you more depth on the screen."

Such a rigid design was unusual in the Disney Studio culture, as was the kind of authority that Walt

had entrusted to the young artist. There was resistance to Earle's new ideas and also resentment toward him because he seemed to dismiss the artistic evolution in animation design that had been accomplished at Disney prior to *Sleeping Beauty*. This film was a departure from previous Disney features, and some of Walt's staff found it difficult to stick to important storytelling traditions while adapting to new design styles.

And like any organisation of artists, conflict over philosophy or style is inevitable. Earle was, by his own admission, confident to the point of arrogance, and his youthful fervour for this all-encompassing design vision no doubt grated on the established artists at Disney. Most of the team had watched *Sleeping Beauty* develop over the greater part of the 1950s, from that first 1952 story presentation and through its various permutations.

Character Conflict

There was also a natural resistance to the *strictness* of Earle's design precepts. For the fairies, for instance, Earle and character lead Tom Oreb had initially designed the characters of Flora,

Fauna, and Merryweather in much stricter geometry to reflect the three primary shapes—square, triangle, and circle. Naturally, this design dictum was a hindrance to the physical process of animation acting, and  it limited the ability of the animators to make the many small design adaptations that were also common in creating an animation performance.

And there's no doubt that Earle's design codes were a hindrance to the animators, who were used to a great deal of design leeway in order to generate the best

Left and above: Maleficent's final costume foreshadows her transformation into a horned dragon.

114

Many versions of the good fairies, including Flora, were explored before artists settled on three little old ladies.

FLORA

performance, and who were used to being the "leading men" as far as the animated features went.

Perhaps because of his skill as a draftsman, Marc Davis (1913-2000) appears to have had the best understanding of the methods of integrating one's work into the "look" of the film. Davis took the limitations inherent in the design and found other ways to enhance the animation performance. His work on Aurora and Maleficent is graphically very strong. For the most part, he used a limited, almost stately *lack* of motion to communicate a seething grace in the wicked fairy, and for all her geometric precision, Princess Aurora is lithe, fluid, and . . . well, *animated*.

According to several sources, the design of the princess disguised as Briar Rose was based on the physical geometry of Audrey Hepburn. The qualities of that actress's slender, willowy physicality lent themselves beautifully to the design environment of the film.

Davis seems to have recognised the design *advantages* of the characters he animated, using their geometry to the benefit of their performance. Briar Rose's hair is a good example of geometry used to communicate dimension. It frames her face, assuring that her features are a focal point and always discernible. As she moves her head, the hair moves in a kind of perspective to give a feeling of depth. Her hair and clothes are designed with vertical lines, to blend with the horizontal/vertical line contrasts of the backgrounds.

Left: Disney veteran Marc Davis was the supervising animator for Aurora and Maleficent. Above: In creating Aurora, Davis was greatly influenced by Tom Oreb's early concepts of the character.

Special Processes

In addition to its distinct production design, *Sleeping Beauty* showcases innovative effects animation and special processes. The process lab at Disney is something of a hidden treasure. The pioneering work that this group had done, beginning with *Pinocchio* and *Fantasia* nearly two decades earlier, was again showcased in *Sleeping Beauty*—techniques involving elaborate camera processes, double exposures, special props, and other technical wizardry. The scenes illustrating the fairies' gifts are remarkable in the way they bring life and motion to Eyvind Earle's static concept paintings.

Distinct Design

Decades later, it is easy to forget what a design departure *Sleeping Beauty* was for Disney animation. The 1950s had seen Disney settle into design with a softness of geometry and lushness of colour in one animated feature after another, from *Cinderella* to *Alice in Wonderland* to *Peter Pan* to *Lady and the Tramp*.

Although each film was visually distinct, none was as startling, perhaps even radical, as *Sleeping Beauty*, to

an audience that had come to expect a certain "house style" in Disney animation.

It has been said that the draftsmanship of this film was executed with such precision and painstaking attention that many of the cleanup artists used protractors, rulers, and T-squares.

Above: Animators Ollie Johnston and Frank Thomas view test animation for the three good fairies on a machine called the Moviola.

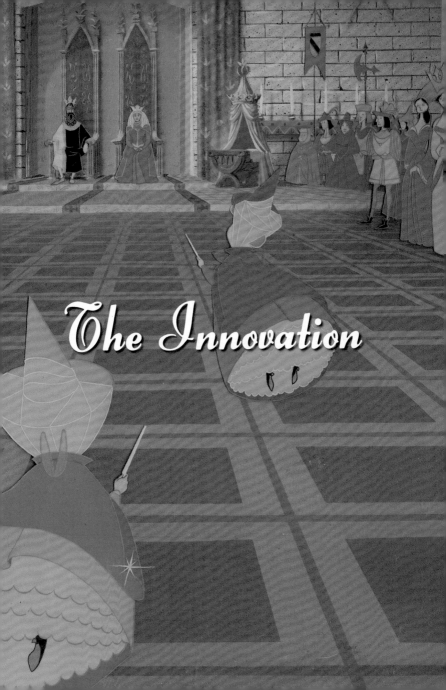

The Innovation

The Innovation

Sleeping Beauty premiered in the era of the Hollywood epic, and Walt Disney brought the animated feature into this epoch through the application of the latest motion-picture production and presentation innovations, such as wide-gauge Technirama 70mm photography and six-track stereophonic sound.

Going Wide

Early on, 35mm film stock with an almost square shape or "aspect ratio," was established as the movie industry standard for exhibition. Experimentation with and showing of alternate, and in many cases superior, film-projection formats occurred regularly throughout the first half-century of movie exhibition.

Widescreen film formats had been around since practically the invention of motion pictures, though, and the exhibition of wide-gauge film had actually

Left: Sleeping Beauty *was created as a widescreen film.*

Eyvind Earle's inspirational images for Maleficent's castle. Earle later commented that his work on Sleeping Beauty was the first time he had ever been paid for his paintings.

begun in earnest in 1930 with a Fox Films 70mm process known as "Grandeur."

However, it wasn't until the 1950s that theatre owners sought out a new and unusual presentation format that led to the development of several wide-screen processes.

Why a wide screen? Because in most ways, a screen with an aspect ratio of 2.5 to 1 and a rectangular shape more naturally duplicates what we actually see. The standard square shape is more akin to looking out a window.

And in the case of wide-gauge film formats, the use of a larger negative simply means more frame area and a sharper, steadier visual image.

In addition, the exhibitors needed to create something new to draw in audiences. Movie attendance in

Above: Walt Disney explains the difference between 35mm film (almost square in shape) and 70mm film (more panoramic).

the 1950s had dropped enormously, as people sought out other diversions and activities and television began to grow in popularity. In addition, the Supreme Court decision to divest the movie studios of the theatres they owned completely changed the way movies were booked around the country.

So, in many ways, widescreen began as a gimmick to draw in audiences. Cinerama was the first widescreen process to debut, but it was cumbersome and limited to specially equipped theatres. With its four projectors (three for visuals and one for sound) and gigantic, deeply curved, 146-degree arc screen, your neighbourhood theatre just couldn't show Cinerama films.

Next, 20th Century-Fox debuted an anamorphic widescreen system that they dubbed CinemaScope. This process used a lens to compress a wide image onto standard 35mm film.

Then there were wide-gauge processes that used bigger negatives, from which prints twice as wide as standard could be struck. These various processes have become known over the years under a generic term, "70mm."

Shape-Shifting

Sleeping Beauty was filmed using this wide-gauge process. A few years before, *Lady and the Tramp* had been shot and released in CinemaScope, but the decision to do so had been made as an afterthought. With *Sleeping Beauty*, the entire production had been designed from the start to take advantage of the wide frame.

Initially, the artists and animators were a little intimidated by the shift in shape. In particular, the layout department had to carefully examine all of the various camera angles, character staging, and movement within the frame to make sure it still looked natural.

It's rather remarkable to look at *Sleeping Beauty* as a whole, however, taking into account the distinct disadvantage the artists were working under as a result of the widescreen format, and see how successful the Disney team was. The final battle between Phillip and Maleficent in particular shows a confident and skilled use of staging, camera angles, and camera movement

Right: Shooting Sleeping Beauty *in a wide-screen layout allowed for more room to show the film's elaborate backgrounds.*

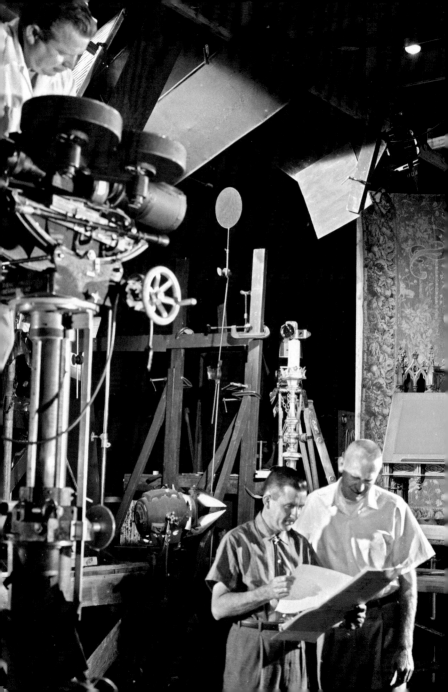

that makes that scene the most exciting and kinetic part of the entire film.

Stereophonic Sound

Another advantage to the development of widescreen was the re-introduction of stereophonic sound to theatres. Walt had experimented with and brought that sound technology to mainstream exhibition in a form known as "Fantasound," for the original release of *Fantasia* (1940).

It is little known that Walt Disney also wanted to employ innovative visuals for *Fantasia*. "At that time with *Fantasia*," Walt Disney told Hooper Fowler of *Look* magazine in 1964, "I wanted to use a wider screen. I wanted to double my screen, and I was all set to do it, but the bankers had their foot on my neck and I had to go along with the conventional. But I still had my stereophonic sound."

Stereo was reintroduced in a more practical incar-

Right: A modernist style was used to portray Prince Phillip's epic journey from Maleficent's castle to the sleeping Princess Aurora.

nation when the widescreen formats were rolled out in
the 1950s, and it was used to provide a corresponding
aural sense of place commensurate with the detailed
and brilliant visual presentation that the widescreen
and wide-gauge film formats and the new super-sized
screens brought to motion-picture presentation.

Having said all that, it is curious that Disney animation abandoned the widescreen format completely
after *Sleeping Beauty*. It wasn't until *The Black Cauldron*
in 1985 that a wide-gauge animated feature would
come from Disney again.

Promotion with Innovation

Walt promoted the release of *Sleeping Beauty* with the first-ever stereo television simulcast and the premiere telecast of film clips in the widescreen "letterbox" format.

On January 30, 1959, ABC's *Walt Disney Presents* (the successor title to *Disneyland* and the precursor to *Walt Disney's Wonderful World of Colour* for the weekly Disney TV anthology hour) offered a stereo broadcast of "The Peter Tchaikovsky Story"—which included scenes from *Sleeping Beauty*—by using ABC-affiliated AM and FM stations for the left and right audio channels.

The film was presented in widescreen using a process Walt called the "Magic Mural Screen," establishing a "theatre" setting and showing sequences in the form we know today as "letterboxing"; the top of the screen was filled with a "house curtain" valance to offer the illusion of a widescreen theatrical presentation.

Left: For two weeks beginning January 29, 1959, the first public screenings of Sleeping Beauty *were held at L.A.'s Fox Wilshire Theatre.*

The Music

The Music

Another reason for the opulent theatrical presentation design for Disney's adaptation of *Sleeping Beauty* was the importance of the musical score in the retelling of the famous tale.

A Musical Beauty

Before Tchaikovsky's unforgettable and beloved version, several ballet productions were based on the Sleeping Beauty story. Italian composer Michele Carafa (Michele Enrico Francesco Vincenzo Aloisio Paolo Carafa de Colobrano) composed *La Belle au bois dormant* in 1825. The opera, with a French libretto, was first performed at the Théâtre de l'Académie Royale de Musique in Paris.

In the winter of 1828–1829, the leading French dramatist of the first half of the nineteenth century, Eugène Scribe, furnished a scenario as a basis for French dancer and choreographer Jean-Louis Aumer's

Left: A 1959 movie poster for Sleeping Beauty.

choregraphy of a four-act ballet-pantomime *La Belle au bois dormant*, which was set by Louis-Joseph-Ferdinand Hérold and first staged at the Académie Royale, Paris, April 27, 1829. Hérold popularised the Scribe piece with a piano *Rondo Brilliant* based on themes from the score, but the ballet was never staged again.

Perhaps the most famous and beloved adaptation of the Sleeping Beauty story is the 1890 ballet score composed by Pyotr Ilyich Tchaikovsky. Although Walt Disney himself initially shied away from the famed Tchaikovsky music for his film adaptation, he realised that the international popularity and musical timelessness of that work was such that its absence would work against his film, and it was the Tchaikovsky score that was finally utilised in—and became an integral part of—the Disney version of the classic tale.

On May 25, 1888, Ivan Vsevolozhsky, the Director of the Imperial Theatres

in St. Petersburg, Russia, wrote to Pyotr Ilyich
Tchaikovsky, suggesting a ballet based on Perrault's
tale *La Belle au bois dormant*. Reportedly, Tchaikovsky
was initially indifferent to the notion of a new ballet,
still stinging from the lukewarm reception of his *Swan
Lake* score eleven seasons earlier. However, he set to
work with Vsevolozhsky's scenario, and the finished
ballet, with choreography by Marius Petipa, premiered

Left: An early concept of Princess Aurora in her peasant clothing.
Above: The music for Sleeping Beauty *was based on Pyotr Ilyich*
Tchaikovsky's 1890 ballet of the fairy tale.

on January 24, 1890, in the Mariinsky Theatre in St. Petersburg. Tchaikovsky's work received more favourable reaction from the critics than *Swan Lake* had, but the composer did not witness his work become an unbridled success in theatres outside of Russia—he died in 1893.

Musical Modifications

In the early stages of work on the Disney version of *Sleeping Beauty*, it had been decided that the familiar Tchaikovsky ballet score would *not* be used in the film. There was a general feeling that the existing score would be a hindrance in storytelling and difficult to adapt to the needs of the film. Walt himself may also have had a residual resistance based upon criticism levelled at him during the release of *Fantasia*, for its adaptations and alterations of classical music to suit the needs of the medium.

But at a story meeting in 1953, Walt himself

Right: George Burns adapted Tchaikovsky's music for the film's most memorable moments, including "Once Upon a Dream."

changed that decision. He said, "Why don't we get someone who can carry a song for us? We need songs—songs roll it, move it. Get the melodies out of this Tchaikovsky music. Here we have something terrific. They've been stealing from Tchaikovsky for years. Here's a chance for someone to legitimately steal from Tchaikovsky!"

George Bruns (1914-1983) was a film composer and well-known arranger for big bands when Walt hired

him for the Sleeping Beauty project. He wrote "The
Ballad of Davy Crockett" and received Academy Award
nominations for *Babes in Toyland* and *The Sword in the
Stone*. He wrote for many Disney film and TV projects
until his retirement in 1975.

"Can you adapt Tchaikovsky's ballet for the film
score?" Walt asked the big, bearish Bruns. "Why not?"
he answered. "I've been rewriting Tchaikovsky for my
own music for years now!"

*Above: King Hubert and King Stefan toast Princess Aurora and Prince
Phillip in song. Right: Reference drawing of the royal minstrel.*

Rewrites, Revisions & Removals

Bruns set about adapting Tchaikovsky's beloved ballet music as the overall score for the film. Lyrics were added to familiar melodies by a variety of writers and became songs, such as "I Wonder," "Once Upon a Dream," and "Hail to the Princess Aurora."

Along the way, many ideas were developed, discarded, or repurposed. Some of the more interesting and notable musical efforts include:

Tchaikovsky's "Silver Fairy Theme." Lyrics were added by Sammy Fain and Jack Lawrence to create the tune "Sing a Smiling Song." It was intended for the three fairies, but used only on record-album releases of the film music.

"Go to Sleep, Go to Sleep" was intended for the castle sleep spell but was replaced by "The Sleeping Beauty Song." "Go to Sleep" held its place in the score into the very last phases of final production. It was performed by the same chorus heard in the finished film, directed by John Rarig, and it lasted the exact

length of the final sequence. However, the melody alone was used during the sequence when the fairies take Princess Aurora back to the castle on the eve of her sixteenth birthday.

"Brothers in Evil" was originally planned to be sung by Maleficent's goons but was not developed further than the demo stage. The music was ultimately used as underscoring in the cottage sequence, when the fairies prepare for Briar Rose's surprise party.

"My Beloved" later became known as "The Love Theme from Sleeping Beauty." There are lyrics credited for this song, but they were never used, even in the commercial recordings. This Tchaikovsky melody plays during the opening narration and after Phillip defeats Maleficent.

Above: Bill Pete's concept for Maleficent's goons was based on medi-aeval castle gargoyles. Right: Eyvind Earle's painting of knights on horseback holding flags inspired the film's opening procession.

Ready to Record

When Bruns was ready to record the score, he was given the freedom to create a worthy companion for the film's opulent visuals. The conductor hand-selected and assembled an orchestra in Germany, where the best state-of-the-art stereophonic recording equipment and sound studios of the time could be found.

Once the score recording and editing was complete, Disneyland Records' creative producer Tutti Camarata enthused to Walt Disney that this magnificent stereophonic recording should be made available to the public, especially considering the new, advanced home stereo systems of the day. More than twenty years before, the soundtrack for *Snow White and the Seven Dwarfs* had set the style and standard of what was known as a soundtrack recording, but it included only the lyrical songs. With *Sleeping Beauty,* Camarata wanted to broaden this notion to include as much of the orchestral score as would fit on a double-sided vinyl 33$\frac{1}{3}$ RPM long-playing record.

With the 1959 LP release of Disneyland STER-4018, *Sleeping Beauty* was also the first soundtrack album

to be issued in full stereophonic sound. "The result helped set the standard for what we now know as soundtrack recordings," says Walt Disney Records producer Randy Thornton.

Bruns's work was nominated for a 1960 Academy Award in the category of Best Music, Scoring of a Musical Picture. The album was nominated for the 1959 Grammy Award for Best Soundtrack Album, Original Cast—Motion Picture or Television.

Sleeping Beauty also represented another continuing Disney tradition. Walt Disney once said, "Music has always played a very important part since sound came into the cartoon. For my medium it opens up unlimited possibilities."

Above: Sleeping Beauty's *album cover.*

The Legacy

NEW 2-DISC PLATINUM EDITION
BLU-RAY™ HI-DEF & DVD

WALT DISNEY
Sleeping Beauty
50TH ANNIVERSARY

NEW
Digital Restoration, Alternate
Opening, Deleted Songs and More.

ONLY on Blu-ray™
"Living" Menus, Exclusive Games
and More.

WALT DISNEY'S ULTIMATE FAIRY TALE!
LIMITED TIME ONLY

The Legacy

Walt Disney's *Sleeping Beauty* was produced in a changing era of Hollywood. Traditional big-studio films vied with intimate human stories, epics competed with small-scale dramas, as the existing studio system tried to adapt to the changes wrought by new technology and a quickly-changing audience demographic.

Television had become commonplace, and owing to this new in-home entertainment (and a variety of other business shifts), movie studios and theatre owners felt the need to create spectacular entertainment for the movie houses, preferably in widescreen and stereophonic sound. In this way, *Sleeping Beauty* was really Walt Disney's "epic" animated feature.

On its initial 1959 release, *Sleeping Beauty* was paired with the innovative live-action "nature symphony," *Grand Canyon*. Carrying on a style originated in Walt Disney's *Fantasia*, this spectacular and unusual

Left: The Sleeping Beauty *poster created for the 2009 DVD release.*

film wed the music of Ferde Grofe's beloved 1931 *Grand Canyon Suite* with spectacular CinemaScope visual images shot on location in the famed western Arizona gorge. Directed by James Algar (who had also directed "The Sorcerer's Apprentice" segment of *Fantasia*), the 29-minute short was an impressive companion to the feature, and it earned a 1959 Academy Award for Best Short Subject, Live Action.

Although greeted with critical praise, and a favourite of audiences, *Sleeping Beauty* failed to earn back its investment on its initial release. A 1970 release sparked curiosity and enthusiasm among Disney fans, but was shown only in 35mm and monaural sound, robbing the film of its visual and auditory impact.

In 1979, a new enthusiasm for widescreen and stereophonic projection was spearheaded by the releases of *Star Wars* (1977) and *Close Encounters of the Third Kind* (1978) in this format. *Sleeping Beauty* was given a limited test engagement at the Crest 70 Theatre in Seattle, Washington, and the enthusiastic audience and critical response and exceptional box-office performance encouraged The Walt Disney Studios to release

the film worldwide in the widescreen and stereo format. The film's innovation and sophistication found a new audience and new regard in the late 1970s, and although a little bit tardy, finally joined the canon of Disney Classics.

Sleeping Beauty has become, through these re-releases, the second most financially successful film released in 1959, second only to another famous widescreen epic, *Ben-Hur*. (When adjusted for ticket-price inflation, the domestic total gross comes out to an astounding $478.22 million, placing it in the top 30 of adjusted films!)

Sleeping Beauty Comes Home

Sleeping Beauty was one of the first Disney animated features released on both VHS and laser disc in 1986

Above: Aurora and Phillip. Artists often drew characters together in the concept stage to see how well they fit with each other.

as part of the Walt Disney Home Video Classics Collection and was the first Disney film released on video to be digitally processed in hi-fi stereo. Although it is difficult to understand today, where a home media release is simply the final venue for a motion picture, the release of a Disney animated feature on video during this time was something of a sensation.

In 1997, the film underwent an extensive and painstaking digital image restoration and was then re-released to both VHS and laser disc as part of the Disney Masterpiece Collection.

It was this restored master of *Sleeping Beauty* that was released to DVD in 2003, in a two-disc Special Edition, complete with a widescreen stereo version of *Grand Canyon*, extensive audio commentary, and dozens of bonus features.

New Technology

For the 50th Anniversary BluRay DVD release of this now-classic animated feature, The Walt Disney Studios Library Restoration and Preservation team undertook an unprecedented restoration. They went all the way

back to the film source: the original black and white successive exposure Technirama camera negative.

(Successive exposure is a method where each finished animation cel is photographed "in succession" on three adjacent film frames through filters for the discrete colour levels—red-green-blue. These separate frames would have then been combined back into a single colour master during printing.)

"Because the Studio employed the SE method for original photography on animation, and due to the double-frame widescreen layout of the Technirama negative, we had to scan more than 7.5 linear miles of

Above: Merryweather and Flora never agreed on the colour for Princess Aurora's royal ball gown.

negative," says Theo Gluck, Disney's director of Library Restoration and Preservation.

Because the original negative was scanned, the team was also able to eliminate the secondary optical step that had to be built into all of the 35mm anamorphic elements that had been used in all prior video transfers, where the image was first compressed and then widened to its original widescreen shape. These scans also revealed that the animation had been completed to a full 2.55:1 aspect ratio (rather than the more typical 2.35:1), revealing additional image area on the far sides of the frame.

As with all of the restoration work done on the new line of Platinum DVDs, the Studio scanned the negative at 4K on an IMAGICA scanner and realigned and composited the images back into colour at 4K. All subsequent restoration work, including cleanup, cel dust and film dirt removal, grain management, and colour grading were all done at 2K.

For accurate colour reference, original 35mm CinemaScope Technicolor dye-transfer release prints were used, as well as surviving cel setups and back-

grounds housed in the Walt Disney Animation Studios Research Library, a process executed on every one of the Platinum DVD editions.

Audio Beauty

"As for the sound," Gluck continues, "we were quite fortunate to still have the three-track stereo 35mm magnetic music recordings that were done by George Bruns in Berlin in 1958. Those masters, along with other audio separations, allowed us to restore not only the original mix, but also create a whole new 5.1 mix,

Below: Princess Aurora sings "I Wonder" in the forest.

and a very special 7.1 mix exclusively for the BluRay disc." For further audio forensics, the restoration team obtained a vintage 70mm print of the film from the East Coast and ran it in the Studio theatre to further their knowledge of the original sound design.

Supplemental Beauty

In addition, restored versions of the classic featurette *Four Artists Paint One Tree* and *The Peter Tchaikovsky Story* (as well as the different, Walt Disney–hosted TV version of "The Peter Tchaikovsky Story") and a new 4K, 5.1 restored upmix restoration of *Grand Canyon* were all completed as a part of the BluRay DVD project.

Happy Endings

As with the heroine of the film itself, Walt Disney's *Sleeping Beauty* has, over its half-century lifetime, been the subject of fond hopes and beautiful gifts, ill will and dormancy, and it has been awakened by the acts of those with a pure love of all her lovely and unique qualities.

May they all live happily ever after!

And they lived happily ever after

And they lived happily ever after.